Ringing The Creativity Bell

Austin Blaine Smith

iUniverse, Inc.
New York   Bloomington

Ringing The Creativity Bell

iUniverse books may be ordered through booksellers or by contacting:

iUniverse
1663 Liberty Drive
Bloomington, IN 47403
www.iuniverse.com
1-800-Authors (1-800-288-4677)

Because of the dynamic nature of the Internet, any Web addresses or links contained in this book may have changed since publication and may no longer be valid. The views expressed in this work are solely those of the author and do not necessarily reflect the views of the publisher, and the publisher hereby disclaims any responsibility for them.

ISBN: 978-1-4401-6207-7 (pbk)
ISBN: 978-1-4401-6208-4 (ebook)

Printed in the United States of America

iUniverse rev. date: 10/7/09

Black Heart...White Blood

Woke up this morning

Past, future, present

Cannon shots exchanged

A Battle at sea between two pirates

Black Heart versus White Blood

Will a flag raise up in victory?

Both the ships are sinking

Below decks the yells are rising

SAVE US CAPTAIN!

Heard from either side

We have families

We have homes

We have dogs

We like green pastures

Why oh why must this battle rage?

Repeating night after night then again and again forever and
after after

We can hear your cries and your laughter

It is you Captain that command these great ships

Why must you keep taking us all out to sea

Do you really have to prove that you are so great?

Do you both think that you are so mighty?

We all have dreams as well

Under your command

We are serving you well

We do what you ask

We load your cannons

With these lead balls

We spill our blood

We accept our fate

We take our falls

So can you not see we are serving you well?

For your glory

You are putting us through a living HELL

Will you please stop this on going tragedy?

Will you please give us liberty?

Ring the bell

Turn the ships around

Sail to common ground

We have all danced before when were children

Now we are at sea and the circle is broken

The waves are crashing at the side of this vessel

It will not be long before we are all washed to sea

Do you really want us all to become a part of your tragedy?

We are begging you Captain

Do not make us fire another cannon

We have asked you more than once now

We want what is right

To be with our families

To enjoy a peaceful clear starry night

Is this asking too much?

Please turn these ships around

We have been asking you night after night

Please take us homeward bound.

The Captains replied at the same time

What if we return

With our heads held high

And receive not a smile

Nor a thankful reply

What will one do

But run back to that boat

Where one can be all alone

This is not what we want

For we love our ship mates

The thought of losing all of you is thought that we hate

Then turn the ships to shore

This they replied in unison

Look to the light

Can you not see the horizon?

Can you not see the sun?

There is not much time before these vessels have taken on too much water

Then we will all be doomed

We will never see our families or our father's

At this moment the Captains looked across at each other

They said this fighting must stop

For we are all sisters and brothers

If we work together

Surely we can bring these ships home

If we work together

We will not have to walk alone

These distant shores

They do not have to be so distant

So in an instant

The sails were raised

In an instant

The Captains received praise

They immediately felt a warmth inside

They immediately felt they no longer had to hide

Everyone on board began working side by side

Everyone on board knew this would be the last fight

The sun kept rising

As it always does

The shore grew nearer

All hands on the ships began to cheer and to sing

They all pinched each other to make sure it was not a dream

Today said the captains

We shall all gather and have a feast

Today said the captains

We have unlocked the beast

6/24/09

Chapter ONE

I stepped out. Before I did, I had to warm up my coffee. I had a cigarette in a garage that had become all too familiar. I'm jumping through doors ahead of time, before I've even taken the elevator to where my golden ride awaited me. Not in weight, only in color. The Golden Chair-O-Ka-Eye. So...I will go back to the beginning. Eggs for breakfast. Eggs, they had taken a whole new meaning recently in my life. This dull cloud had settled, and hung so low it's a wonder I could see, even with a powerful prescription wrapped around this rubber outer coat. Breakfast sausage and eggs mixed with chit-chatter, no time for pancake batter. He said it himself. "You better get busy." Hell awaits for those who fall. In that case I better get busier, damn busy! Off to the races. Though there are many, it is one combined. May we try like hell to have a good time. Contribution is the solution. Chemistry is not just for men in white lab coats. I wear one now, and I am trying like mad to make a gust of wind take me up, up, up, and away so it will flap with a fury. Let's ride.

Chapter two

A city full of sin? Aren't they all? Aren't we all? Scared to take the fall, but where to? If you have ground that you are standing on, then isn't it you that decides the direction you are going to walk? To step out. A two step shenanigan. Without remorse. I don't think so. Not this picture show. Pine trees are fresh. My apartment was a mess, but when wasn't it ever really? Surface clean I was once told. She was right. Circular patterns. Slices of life. Eagles can fly high, if they dare. I've seen it before. Those who do, usually win. Back to stepping out. One load down. A trusty companion well behaved. Trust. Finish the packing process. Easy, due to the fact that my lazy body, and overdrive gear had kept me from unpacking from my previous misadventure. Looking back, I think all adventure could be summed as misadventure, otherwise how could it really be called an adventure. If there is nothing missed then there is nothing gained right? Right. Wrong? I have two arms. I am this lucky. Thank you. So… I will keep writing. I know we have a constitution. Thank you…So…I will keep writing. I have a brain with many wires. Who knows where they connect or lead to, but I have one. Thank you. So…I will keep writing. I have a heart, I just checked twice and felt it beating. Thank you. I have a family that has put up with way too much SHIT.

Though I am in their home at this moment. Thank you. The friends that I have, same goes for them, I have made errors in the past like a computer that has been submerged in water for days, yet somehow still operates.

Thank you. To everyone that goes to work and has a job. Thank you. To everyone that does not. Thank you. To everyone for being themselves. Thank you.

Chapter #3

(to the highest)

This little bit is to any of you out there wondering where in the gosh dern' tootin heck to hell, and then make a loop again and come back to the start. What is it that I am writing? Where are we going on this journey. Honestly, I can't say, or better yet, write. I will say this much though. If you do not like it and you are thinking of tossing it. Cool. If you will, at least think about this bit of trash I am throwing at you before you stay or go. If ya' think it is trash then why don't you either pass it on to a friend, a library, or re-cycle it. I have been called a re-psycho by my father. I was pretty extreme I will admit. Not that I don't re-cycle anymore, I just need to accomplish. Otherwise I will always re-cycle the same patterns in my own life that I have been doing for far too long. This boy wants to be a man. Move on without a conveyor belt system running underneath my feet as it has been this way for far too long. Do no want to crawl back into a womb. Re-birth. Born-again. New day. Everyday. Ta-taa and toot-a-loo. I hope. Chew-chew-choo.

Chapter ↓

I once had a somebody, we will call them two. Maybe even three, or four would probably be more fitting. I have a key, so we will unlock this door. As I said, it seems rather fitting. They were all manufactured in plants. One sent from a plant straight from his mother. Rode in on a bike rather nonchalantly. Blew in with a gust, not on a breeze. A cool one though. Too cool. Property claims and finances can be a brother or a bother. Back to the friends and where they were manufactured. One from a mother with possible wicked intentions and the other from a place we will call Kalamazoo. A friend that could be replaced for the amount of a dollar sum while the balance of truth was placed on the other. Dynasties have pride. Nothing wrong with that. As long as they have it in the right places. I like to look at the lions whenever I get a chance to visit the zoo. Such strength, power, and beauty. They know all about pride. This is why they form their own. Back to the dynasty. I have always noticed chandeliers that hang when you enter. What are they their for anyways? Just so they can look pretty I presume. Or could it be that they are waiting for the fall. I took a fall. We will call it the forty dollar master what is in your wallet priceless fall. The knot on the tree could not have been finer, and closing the eyes shows my belief system had been where it always has been. As was my heart. My pride! The fourth degree can get hot sometimes, if you stick around and let it burn you. Turn your stereo system up to number 33 and look up. Who is there to catch you now? Oh, the zoo. Yes, makes me think about a date awhile back. Kings and Queens and lions, the tigers, and polar bears. A car was a mess and had been cleaned like the rest. I will bid you farewell for all you have to do is turn the page. Though a cup off coffee takes a bit longer. Be back in a few. Actually, I never left...yet. A conversation took place in the course between now and the cup of jobe, which has not even been brewed as of yet. Though, I will tell you this. Inventions are really cool. I especially like the ones that have been made to carry mankind to higher ground. Not the kind meant to make individuals fall. I have created made up stories before in my mind when I was scared of getting into trouble or not belonging. I realize know that we have to work so hard to not fall. Each and every one of us. This battle rages everywhere. The zoo is not just a place to visit in the city, but it can be in your mind if you want to create it. Outside your font door, if you let it enter your bubble when you walk outside it. Be cautious not to burst any other bubbles that may float your way. We must try to keep the slop in the pig pen, they love it. I love pigs. Bacon tastes good, and the pork is the flavor. For those of you that do not like pork, or do not eat meat. I hope I have not offended you. If I have, then pretend you did not read what you just did. Good day, and now I will go make that cup of coffee. Thank you.

Chapter Jive

The second load has been carried to the wagon. The wheels, the steals, the two bit deals. There is a lot of care in our senior citizens, and there should be. They have a wealth of information that many have turned into knowledge along the way. This can be passed onto the youth of whatever nation they hail from. Whether it be Cambodia or Timbuktu. Though I find the true importance in this world are the children. If they are not raised to have a heart filled with the right pride juice then the apple is going to go sour. When the grape falls from the vine it will shrivel up, and die a slow death that is agony like the rest. Will it be able to pass along a value system of information that can be turned into knowledge or a system that is used only for the gain of power and self interest. Sandpaper is great for taking a piece of wood and making it smooth. What will one accomplish though if you if you rub two pieces together? You will only wear both of them down until there is nothing left and then what? There is light at the end of...WOW! Did you ever notice the way things can be arranged at times in such an odd manner. Almost like it was an arrangement of some sorts. Never fear, look at the ground that you are walking on. You can feel it right? So...keep walking...one foot in front of the other. Stay grounded.

Touch and feel, both physically and emotionally. The wheels in this wagon are now backing up. Just not too far. Out of a gate, and then to the open road. Let it ride with the trusty furry companion by the side. Ooowww! Howlin' and off to the race through a long night of living and dying through hills of laughter and sorrow. Progress being charted by the global return and a re-run of a mid life crisis plays on the windshield of victory. Loss is just as easy to gain, but you have to do the right thing. Driven with the intention of trying to do the latter, there are many that think they are your chief editor in life. What tree did they fall from? Were they swinging from a branch when you looked to the tree for a banana. Why didn't they throw one to you instead of trying to seek out something they could find on their own. Ring, ring…communication. Uh oh, my only form for touching, reaching out with besides my voice. My electronic device is not in my eyesight. Panic? No. Pullover and a quick check on a wing and a prayer is golden in all its splendor. Thank you. Take to the black top one more time though a detour this way and that will make this an excursion in itself. Lost? Not exactly, just for the time being. Hamburgers, I like 'em. There are some boys out there that can grow to become mighty big in size and stature, though this stop there is only enough time for fuel and a relief of inner vinegar. Put the fire out and send that bit to the core. I have heard that there are seven in that mixed up place, and I would not want to find out. Only if there was a guide that could help take me skiing. This winter I would love to check this resort out in a four corner region of the good 'ol home of the free and land of the brave. If I am going to be headed that direction then I will try and write that on the calendar. Traveling. I love to do it. We can travel such a distance now days with these techno advances. I mean if you think about it, we really have achieved time travel haven't we?

The highway...back on it. Even though I am really on a bed heading back to a garage for a cigarette. Now we are really talking about time travel 'eh. At times it can feel like you are a hockey puck that is traveling with the speed of a Bobby Hull slap shot. Will you make it to the net? Better yet, will you score a goal. Take the steps and find out, so history can unravel, and the story will be told. Drawing conclusions can be a basket full of illusions. I like Easter egg hunts. The baskets can come out filled with protein, or they can be empty. Better than something that isn't really there though. The children that go and run around in circles alone usually come away sad. If you pair up and work in a team who knows what you will find. Even if you are lacking protein in the basket, you may have possibly gained a friend. We will chalk this one up as a win, and call it pro-team instead of protein. How about that. Let's put one up on the scoreboard for now. I hope.

Chapter Six

Back to the road and back to the tricks. Not magic. Just trying to avoid any trickery or ballyhoo that may be played. I like to play. Games are fun on a board when everything is laid out for all to see within a circle. The Cherokee is gaining speed and the ground is getting chewed up. The race is on. Against who? My trusty companion knows more than I. For he is my guardian, and keeps a close eye on me when I walk, talk, sleep, and especially when I eat. Have you ever tuned into a radio station and felt like the songs were being played for you and only you? They're not. It still feels really cool though. That is what they are wanting, trying to accomplish when they do what they do. This is what I imagine. I will tell you that this imagination we have, let it run wild dear brother. This is our one way we can truly be free, so let freedom ring dear brothers and sisters. Because you know it is ticking away. Throw in these dern' cigarettes and the other toxins in our midst, and we form another form of this freedom thing again. Uh oh. I think another guitar chord has been struck. Can you hear the tune. I should like to go listen to Hendrix for a bit now. Thank you for the I-Pod. The apple was once bitten and I am more than shy, so why shouldn't we indulge. Groovy little device really. I am surprised it took me so long to come around to it.

All my cd's stored up in one unit. Awesome! Back on the road. Flying like a jay bird and stopping for fuel couldn't be finer. You can find all kinds of neat little treasures in these petrodollar stations that abound this countryside. I picked up a three dimensional lion picture. ROAR! That is what it did to me when I walked by. It did not scare me though, more like it called my name. It was very neat to say the least, so that is all that I will say. Walked the trusty hound and let him sniff around, while I kept looking back over the shoulder. Left and right. For what you are probably wondering? Me too. Could be anything. Aren't there those poisonous lizards out this way? That must be Arizona, but one must be careful on the open road. Misadventure is full of well, misadventure. At times I am wrapped up so tight a kitty cat would mistake me for a giant ball of yarn. Not very big on cats. I love kittens. Batwoman can come over anytime. Cats are kind of spooky to me though. Possible warning sign, or maybe just my overworked imagination. Who knows, the more I seem to find out, the less I really seem to find out. It really is starting to make it tough at times. One step in front of the other brother. Carry on. The thirst, always so thirsty at this point of my travels. Makes me feel like a cowboy on horseback in where else, but the desert. Could it be that is because I am driving in the middle of one? Yes. I am. I have a good air conditioning unit going though, and it isn't even on at full blast. Makes me feel good. My hound too. He is at rest in da' back of da' ca'- and baby we gonna' travel by the moon, and we gonna' travel so far. A little rhyme. He he he. Fun.

Ooowww! Not only are we traveling under the moon, we like to howl at it too.

Rock on! Rolling. The power of soul. I love Jimi. He had it. Thank you.

Chapter 7

Recently passing through this city full of machines with slots and flashing lights I have felt danger signals. Creepy vibrations coming at me from all around like the animals must have been when they were trying to climb aboard the boat before the flood. Take it out of cruise and drive like the dickens. Leave this one behind. Thank you for the lead in my foot. I used to be thrilled when on my way, now I am chilled and that is all I will say. Good day and good night and we always keep to the light. Light bright. What an extraordinary little creative spark that was. Thank you. Uh oh. It is taking me back to Vegas. We are lost, aren't we. Lost eggs even when found still need constant nourishment. The one's that are cracking, or have split wide open must be saved from the frying pan. I think. Maybe, just maybe they need to be scrambled. Who knows. The more you know, the less. I don't know. A laser show would be a cool event right now. I will close my eyes and remember a few from the past. That is something that I will not leave behind. Laser shows are cool. Thank you.

Chapter Ate

Who do we appreciate? LOVE. I like it. Who wouldn't? Pulled over at an almost out of date petrodollar station that is almost as old as the fuel it sells. Water the dog. Ring…ring…ring. This phone seems to ring. Out of the dark. A possible tail. Attached to what though. How could this caller seem to call at moments when one least needs the call. Hmmm. Like a bass in the Ozarks, the fish was hungry, took the bait and ate it. Rather shall we say, it hooked the fish. Though the fish shook free and jumped out of the water. Freedom. How long will it last? Keep the feet on the ground, but learn to fly. Which is a good reminder. Must keep it closed otherwise the animals will run free from the barn. Wouldn't want to scare the old ladies, or turn them on for that matter. Well it actually depends. We will leave it at that. For now. Appreciation. So many things to appreciate, even the things that hurt. Like that bee…that made me…look like an alien. Calm like the sea would have been the proper manner to address the situation, instead of a smack to my outer layer. Though I've always had a ringing in my mind that may never go away. Getting knocked in the noggin' can knock some sense into you. I think it might have to happen in the form of an accident though. Dreams are really fun. So is Disney Land. California is cool. I am tired. Goodnight. Or...maybe not. Mine would be a tough eyelid down opener. Virgins drifting off the road from glaring headlights and floating down a river. Beauty that can not be bought nor sold, a treasure from sweet June. A day for a Father if one can make it through a pass with a winding future. Do not fall back. Shut eye for a moment or two. A scruffle and a shuffle on the top and a massage of the ears. Time to travel and go back in history through the years. Keep those robots and monkeys filled with gadgetry and bananas. I am chasing the darkness so I can find this love that has always been and is still there, and is about to be. Shatter those dreams of so called insanity. A verse to those who wait. The dark ages are still here. Can we all share a martini now? Thank you.

Number 9

A fish fry. A gathering. The people sway. The peop
can dance. They can chant if they so please, they si
if they feel the disease. LOVE. It is in the...everywhei
Can you taste it. I just ate an orange, but that w
over two days ago, I am just remembering it rig
now. Actually I just ate a couple of quick bites frc
a hot dog in a bun fresh out of frigate. The attenda
made it seem like it was an out of the way favor wh
asking for a bun. THANK YOU VERY MUCH TOO. H
dogs at petrodollar stations are no longer on th
menu. On to greener grass and finer dining. By th
way I love simple rhyming. Cloud number nine, a tru
friend indeed if you ever need to get higher. Well the
we must all try to aspire to truly get higher, and n
on some cheap thrill, but on a community pill. Ca
it a miracle drug. I was sent a dog to help guide m
on my journey through the seven gates and exile
a lonely place. I shouted and I screamed. I assure
was no dream. I would hope not, though I wish it was
Maybe this is why I still have my moments of sorrow
That current is no longer speeding at such a forc
like it used to. Inclines. Hills. Climb. Used to. Nov
my Cherokee is past that Saint, and a town that goe:
by the name of George. Thank you. Okay. Eyes car
not take it any longer. Must pull over and rest now

The kryptonite...weakness...steering wheel...pulling in different directions...can't ...keep control much longer. Great. A Shell station. Symbolic. I will crawl in the back next to my trusty companion and sleep for days like a turtle in a shell. It was only an hour and a bit more but that was enough to keep the black spirits from making much progress on my tail. Luckily I have a short one too. Thank you. Since I happen to be in a bed at this point I will hyper travel back in time when I wake up and finish where I left off. Slices of life can be like a good piece of pizza, or a bad piece of karma. Sometimes it's instant, and an hour later you are left with heart burn, or it may be years down the road and you are left with nothing. I smoked a joint with a financially troubled man in a vegetative area behind my dwelling one day. He was nice, I hope he is ok. Thank you.

Chapter TEN

I have heard about a group down, or up. I guess it depends which way you are coming from. Either way it is in Greenwich, it as an association. They are courteous and they are a leadership placed here today to conquer all through compassion and caring. Call it bullets of love. Flower power if you will. I will, and I shall. There is also a pond, and in the springtime it blossoms, though it is golden throughout all the seasons. Do not ask for a rhyme for there are too many reasons. Play hard, rest easy. Go boating on cool waters when you get the chance and if a nice lady asks you, then accept the offer and move to the floor and dance, dance, dance. To turn this down will throw confusion in the air and you will be left wondering, you might even swear. A tear drop may fall from one's eye. It may not be from your eye that you are looking through at your moment of truth, but it may come back to haunt you this much I know is true. Eagles are free and we can be too. They are the symbol of America. WOW! Isn't this where I am. My feet are on the ground in this promised land. Enjoy blue rivers and nights on the towns. Hike or bicycle, just move around. A couch can be fine when one is at home, but if that is where you stay you will turn into a bag of old bones. Get out, get out, wherever you are. Sandy bottoms lead to a distant shore. Surging runs and breathtaking leaps, off-road paths are not meant for lack of effort or midnight creeps. A booby prize will be handed out for those who despise, best fighter can be given to those who want to fly. Forces armed with love are on the trail of the white dove. They are pushing higher, an entire division is growing in number and in strength. They are looking good and are ready to cash in at the banks. That golden round pond that shines throughout the seasons, there can only be one true reason. LOVE. Thank you.

Chapter Eleven

A mountaineer sitting atop a ranch, performed a chant while doing a dance. For what? It will remain a mystery, but only one knows what force inside was beaming out. The cosmos rained for days into his soul. The stars came down and melted through the egg. Filling the mind with a course in simple matter, then chickens started to chitter-chatter chitter-chatter. Rock and Roll was forever born. Bells were whistling and a star was born. New planets and cosmos are bursting with energy. They keep on working, they absorb through the light. Call it a braking system throughout the day and into the night. Company is to be cherished even when held to tight, but one must let go if the feeling is not right. A braking system has been put in place to help reach one's mark, to help find the way when lost in the dark. Do not surrender when the way can't be found. For this is surely to drag one under to the cold dark ground. Do not climb a ladder meant for a gorilla. A peak is the place for a de-icing warmth to get rid of the chiller. A teacher that laughs at one's repeated mistakes, is only laughing at there own puffed up flakes. A mirror is a handy gadget device. This is surely a process that can take away the ice. The descent to the dungeon can be for a day, or for more. The harder one laughs, the colder the floor. A student with inner strength will battle back and show up for more. A master of disguise can lead a class into laughter, until the will of one subject tumbles. Rejected to wilt away and let the drops of tears fall. Objection your honor, this cycle can not repeat, who is this that judges to make oneself feel complete. Assembling an army to build one's strength. Due to the lack of one's own inner strength. WHOOWAH! HOORAY! A day of sunshine. Sunshine, sun rain, sun storm, once again. A foot path will lead those who are in need to a place with cool water and treasure abound. A steady course can keep you out of the ground. Look ahead, do not look down. Cast your fly, there are maps in the sky. Once again, let the purple worm fly. One step leather care are for those who want to win. Condition and cleanse. Set sails to a breeze, watch out for coconuts that can fall from the trees. Birds can fly high, but there will always be thunder and rain. Let it rain and let it rain from April to June. Let it thunder and lightning in through the gloom. Nantucket has filled their bucket with oil from a whale. A market with flowers has no need for water from a can. Can you hear the whispers from the classic medium roast man? Peter moss is rich, on the first day of summer. Try not to look down on those who have trouble breathing from down under foot. Condensation will dry up an almost dry lake bed. Take heed and take warning otherwise the fish will wear no head. Eyeballs have protein. So does the yoke. Move through the water with a simple breast stroke. A street with a sack on a river running through fifth avenue. It may do you well if you carry a canoe. A paddle for one would be dandy, but if you look in your pocket. Do not be surprised. A piece of strawberry hard candy meant for two, can make another paddle jump out of the blue. A welcoming party may be in order. So lift up that menu, and place an order. Make a call with your short wave radio. Get on your horse and buggy system and head to the rodeo. Elephants are dancing in the cool summer and winter breeze. Circus tricks are being performed with cowboys that get down on their knees. They have pistols, seven shot revolvers. We have soldiers of love, calling on you. Pick where you are at, and dawn that white striped leather. Pick up a baseball bat. Go hit a homer. Baby, baby I hear the wind blow. Baby, baby the smell of a radio and the volume is growing louder. No more dark clouds can pound and shake around. The horses are calm though they are wild at heart. Off to the races they are all playing and ready to ride. Give them a saddle, a harness too. Hang on tight, off to Kalamazoo. Ammaramadonnaoomommamommacoolwaterflowdownasunderfromupundertotothebackuptheheadsurewouldmissyaifyouweredead. Thank you.

Chapter Twelve

Roots can replenish and process contemporary pineapples. A glove for a body will fit and provide one with oxygen through a snorkel through a system of parks. As was said before do not get lost in the dark. Out standing on an island in the middle of harmful solvents. Go shopping for nutrients not animal by-products. Natural color, a rainbow after rain. Now three hundred and eighty cups meant for pleasure not pain. Cast for excitement and correct your spelling. Tell a tale of goodwill and you may be invited. A key stone, a misadventure. Wouldn't want to miss ya' on this misadventure. Myrtle grass on a sandy beach by a river shore. I am sure there is a tail attached I just can not gather more. The seeds they drop and yes they grow. Two lanes intersect. A division can grow, but this one can unite. It is up to individuals to throw out the dice. Laughing man crow will surely tell all. It is not just a game if you look into the eyes of a bull. A lamb will shake. The earth may quake, do not hesitate. The bus may come late, or not show up at all. Carry on and bark like a hound. Let it carry and resonate with sound. Shift into high gear for we are land riders. Intelligent vehicles that can buff and polish. Swinging in tune to a squirt with cycles. Sausages that are tasty, some enjoyed with mustard. Hose for carrying fluid,

Allen could not be flustered. Swinging from a rope, looking cool for all to see. Say it again. Cuss in front of an elder, one who carried a babe in a womb. With nonchalance, who carried who on a broom. A bastard child sat outside a door. A screen filled with pictures of violence and horror. Comedy comes in many forms and delight. The choice is there for the taking, it is up to one to decide what is right. A mouse trap filled with cheese can be a disease. Though if one can be quick it may not fall prey. A repetition process is not meant to repeat day after day. Echoes are meant to carry on through a valley. If stuck in a mind cobwebs will form. Then you be locked outside a dorm. Running on a real field catching passes made up of a football in one's dreams. Could it really be it is all as real as it seems? Green emeralds shimmer like a lake made of gems. Mojo, Tojo, toe jam, glisten listen, heartbeat, thunder, bang. One hundred and ten percent should be repeated again and again. Shortcuts can work, if done the right way. To walk around a mountain may lead to a sunny day. A rocky road can eventually lead to a steep incline. Though a rocky ledge may bare and yet hold many vines. Grammar and grade school can be a project. Ceramics can be honey for an oven document. Beaches surrounded by a Hamilton Cove. It was in a fort that one took a chance and unlocked a master. Old English leather and classic solitude will no longer lead to disaster. For now we will call the master the blaster. A kneel to sun. A forest piano. A country instrumental performed in the shadow. Can you escape the grips of someone who knows what your after? An answer from a wizard, do you want truth? Those who can not accept will bare the excuse. Flight patterns and zigzags are ramps to disaster. A burden is meant for the core, and the key is not handed to unlock the door. The grain in wood. Time will tell. Lines of grey. I can hear the bells ring, and I can hear the salesman sell. I can trade this and I can trade that. Just be sure to give me, give me, give me and we will call it just that. Lighthouse keeper, please keep that light bright. For there are many vessels trying to make it through the night. Corn husks need husking, so one feed on the plenty. We must make sure that there is always plenty. Enough with bottom rooms and buffaloes from the East. Billy the Kid traveled the West and tried his best to be a regulator of peace. A basin in a forest filled with snow. Strap on boards to glide far and wide, a remarkable formula to feel the glide. A bridge across water. A miracle in itself. We are walking across water on our own memory shelf. Selfish. Fish. Swim upriver. Tumble back. It couldn't be quicker. Thank you.

Chapter Thirteen

Apply in direct sunlight. A mountain grown formula. Definite desire to stay. Biting and fighting all of the way. A lodge in a corner. A burner set to high degree. Pull thru tool box and a hand in water set for placement to grab what is in need. Country of origin? Unknown. Whistle stop tour to a land before time. A melodious howl from the trusty companion that had been in a cage for a long time. A mark in a hall. Gold crown to be worn. For who? Checkout time is a three night minimum. A walker with wheels can cost a premium. Unleaded fuel and many stops along the way. Kung fu and Karate are martial law in a finer way. Balance an art. For there are many. Hold fast and set sail to the shore of plenty. Blue and yellow stripes wind down a cord. A standard swan river, a seasonal fjord. Start using wax and words and the rhymes. Fireworks boom and they lit up the skies. A three month lease on this no reservation Saturday. Let the children go, and let the children play. Preferred filtration with candles that surround. A sandy beach fire meant to sing and gather around. Thank you.

Chapter Fourteen

There was a wall of rock. Built from many. I touched it. I felt it. I climbed a part of it. It was real. Taste. Pure. Rich. Weekly memorials. Tents latched onto trailers. Garages parked in homes with signs having sales. A man walked to a door with something to deliver. He said excuse me Mam. I think you need to sign my paper. Without hesitation a scribble was scratched down. A patter down the pavement as his feet hit the ground. With a rumble keeps on working. Baggage filled with clothing though not in tatters. Meant for those less fortunate that have not been able to gather. Needs are common. All have them. Working together is chemistry. Glasses filled with solutions. SCUDS make attacks. Patriot inventions. Select a size and there may be a surprise. Open your gift and see what is inside. Protection products. Sewer systems carry waste. Played as a pawn. Telescoping heights. Early morning dawn. Must rent a second site. Then go and learn from the first. A garage filled with classic cars till the ego bubble bursts. History foundation. Bringing up the past. A stick that has been left. A leaf overturned. A dying fading breath. A store with name for convenience in a state of western local does not accept the cowboy honor code. Greed and corruption has disrupted and the volcano overflowed. A visit out of need, but no longer if one can help it. Cancerous ways are only going to dissolve. Yeast can rise with the right mixture. A room full of lies will paint a black picture. Contact with the eyes. A loaf pan for bread. Irritation in my eyes. Give me olive oil for the irritation. Tear off the cloth. Wipe the water from the basin. Unbleached the flour. Sea salt for a friend. Over the hill under foot. Carry a weight. Our palate craves a shady brook. Polar star. Nautical adventures. Water temperatures in the sixties. Take us back to the flower sixties. Yellow. Lethal threat. Junior card deck. A skateboard on a tiger run. A valley save everything guide. Who will drop the gun? A map for adventure. A map planned out for fun. A pine tree has grown at least one foot since the last visit. Insulating tape to shelter voltage. Save electrification from reaching the outer layer. Human magnification. Eyes wondering alone. A knife carving a piece of meat. Meant for the plate to be taken home. Feasting on berries with morning dew. One must say. Salt and sulphur and mercury. Together it can rise. Shelter from a storm. Hail can pound. A dent on the roof. Bark on the tree. A child with glee. Mother with open arms take in thee.

Chapter Fifteen

Smell the coffee? I can't. The coffee tastes good though. I can see the road to victory. Always been a favorite of mine. NASCAR. I seventy zero we will call this one a hero. Hero status in my book due to the beauty and all the great places it has taken me. Also the places it can lead to. Snowy peaks throughout all the seasons. To not show emotion would be an act of treason. I will travel as the speed signs allow. Kick into cruise, and let the wagon take control. Let it roll, we shall let it rock if you like. The blues. I know of a butterfly that flutters by with a sweet grace that can pick one up whenever feeling down. This sweet soul helped me out when I was feeling down. Eyelids are still tired, though the mind is feeling wired. Watch out there may be deer or elk crossing, and they may to be wired. In a different way of course. Beautiful. Thank you. Hairs on back are standing up and I have to go if you know what I mean. Can't take the overload. Devil's Canyon. No place I would rather piss some vinegar with my trusty companion by my side on a nature walk than in a canyon with a name like this one. Symbolic Native American Jewelry was bought from a long distance runner. She had my heart pumping from her kind words and sincerity. This is a great nation. For any of the pigs that do not believe in generosity and man kind, may they sit where my dog and I pissed our vinegar. X marks the spot. Send it to the core. Hand bags. There are many. I have my luggage in the back, and a lot I would rather not talk about. Push on to colorful. First we must make way down a river of greenery. Never really been very green to me though, but oh well. Buckets of ice do not wash car windows well. Canyons of rabbits are pretty much nothing but canyons. For those rabbits are rascally, for I do not believe I have ever seen any out of all the times I have been through this particular area. A fruiting of nature and hamburgers for my hound. Dinosaurs walking risen from the ground. A walk in a park in the light, and not in the dark. Blue sky nature fresh air, just what was needed to take us the rest of the way there. Mick mack mick macks chimed the little boy from out in the distance, Wendy I think you charge too much said the great spirits. Around the round about we fled from this nature preservation. Look to the right and we pass the last reservation. Golden Cherokee travel fast to the destination. Only one more stop at one last petrodollar station. Big rigs Irish jigs cross the Continental Divide. Out of the mountains the eyes can now see far and wide. At last at last fall to the floor close the eyes now it is safe to snore. Thank you.

Chapter Sixteen

Suburban book of blues biggest construction in the undertaking. Hot coffee pad red flag warning. A sonic boom blast can reach tired poor mans deaf ears. Protection from the watchers, but are they in the bleachers? Gold meadow birds swerve to avoid the midnight creatures. Will you remember the little things when it has all been said and done? Emergency assistance, or a hardened shackle lock?. Tick tock tick tock tick tock went the clock before the bell was struck. A moody afternoon was spent day dreaming down by a river. Chasing clouds in ones mind could not be finer. Lamp shades meant to shade only blotted out the memory of ones past lover. A phonograph on a table played, but the neighboring stereo system only played their music louder. Telephones rang throughout the middle of the night. This is when the sun came back in and woke the boy into a man from a long awaited slumber. Sweat drenched. How could one have spent so many nickels and dimes so carelessly, and in such a fashionable manner. Sit down now said the cricket, it is time to enjoy a rather fine dinner. Thank you.

SEVENTEEN

Love is hate. Hate is love. Once said the cricket to the high flying white crow. Did I rattle your cage? I will tell this story about a song horse that ran through the night with blinded white rage. Harassed throughout the night by the caped marauder that wore a mask from an unmarked age. A turnip with of an off colored shade marked the paint of an old war machine that had seen better days. Triumph or defeat one can not tell, but if you look closely you will see. There may be a certain storm brewing that could bring inner tranquility. A brewers yeast, overall coats and arms in muck to the elbows with grease. A greedy mouth opened wide, before given a feast. The journey had almost ended in a purgatory bliss. Then hells thunder struck on the forehead, and sent the sail ship into a whirlpool. Down a steady decline into the deep abyss a tragedy about to repeat though is it justice or could this be a payback whip that may have missed? Target snapped and the oil painting is still wet. Many lessons learned yet the eyes are not wet. Oceans storm often, and calm even when it's full moon. Ball bounce in other's courts even in a crowded room. Familiar faces can go unnoticed even from a watchful eye. This is why a shake of the tail from the squirrel shook. A chip from the chipmunk chunked. The ball will bounce and the laundry is waiting to dry. Selfishness a lesson in this chapter that is more than meets the eye. Thank you. You are welcome. No I insist, Thank you.

eighteen

No significance in being kept in the loop tonight, only that the cuckold was growing wiser by the minute, and bellbottom hippies drew rainbows with crayons on the sidewalks. Dogs would pass by in the shadows rapidly at glance. Then in one instant the peacock drew her feathers, and began her elegant dance that would entangle the spirited mind of the once forgotten youth. A new chapter was being formed and an ill forgotten past rushed to the shore on a surf pattern. The midnight roar of the canyon river passed by with bees vibrating from the taste of nectar. A sweet delicate frozen waterfall. A siren with a sudden stop. Held hostage by a demon. Living down on the corner of the next block. Snail pace laundry run in the wee morning hours. If you can catch a ticket to the railroad station there will be a peach tree girl with flowers in her hair. Grey star showdown at a local track. A swimmer attacked alone. Great white shark attack. Zero zip tolerance for a toothbrush without a comb. If you need a cavity I will give a roll of cavity hard candy causing cheese. Trying to sail a sail ship, but the battleship brings the people to their knees. Forty inches of hubble on the double, and one can float to the outer limit. If you say cheese in the wrong direction some SELFISH MONKEY PRICK MAY TRY AND DOCUMENT YOU IN IT! THUNDER

ON THESE SOULS! THESE NAMELESS JOHN FUCKING DOES! Machinery and business talk with numbers that add up to something, yet when looked upon in the greater skeem make one drunk with foolish rage that can drag down a dragon. Throw it to the pits and to the core. Let their lies and tomfoolery die on the killin' floor. A love for the blues sent from the heavens, bleeding heart cries out for more. Hear all the round circle chants sweet melody maker. I know you listen to the childish creator. A sandbox on a hill can so easily crumble. A hill can be climbed, though a football can be fumbled. The creativity bell rang, and the forecast looked humble. Inner strength? The lonely lion walked through the desert. Returned to the abode it had begun to inhabit. Crawled back inside a cavity for further research. The bells kept ringing. Further research. Study. Study. Study. Dig up dirt. Sift through the soil. Tired hands lift up evidence. An arrowhead cuts. Blood drips and moistens the already wet soil. Hatred can ruin a city. The walls made of stone can begin to crumble. Set free the birds in a cage. Unwrap the venison from the foil. A plot that thickens with the growing sunlight of each dying day. Again the chants from the village are repeated. John Doe and business talk, commotion set in motion. Singing to a yellow moon. The lost boys tears kept falling from the Heavens. A latch trying to hang itself on a door that has already been securely fastened. The tribal beats now grow in strength and number, the tender foot will not be drug asunder. BEAT IT! The drums POUND! BE GONE. Those who have gathered around in the circle are now calling. Voices raising the roof that does not cover as the heavy rains pour out from their beating hearts. Disco they go go wop wop bop bop your head bang bang your dead you selfish arrogant mother fucker! The stereo booms poolside! A gift given that was asked for! Though the lion was not an Indian giver. Luck has run out for this careless individual may his grave be his forward thoughts for his remainder. Blues extravaganza! A hungry hound and a quick walk around the block. A short race in the race of life down one 0 one to one thousand block for a promised chicken dinner. Upon arrival where was the bird? Still in the freezer. You done me wrong and you ain't no brother. Nothing more than a stereo type THORN! Did I mention the stereo you had time to set up, as the cub took you along you short fingered stickler. Dragons have become such a drag. Go and cry to your yellow moon and pay your musicians well. I will sell you a sweet little tune the first goes like this, "May you rot in HELL, HELL, HELL." Which way will it be? Only you can erase the tragedy of fate which you have stirred. Short little walks and chit chatty talks make tired bones melt from broken words. Yet airplane bombers still fly with bombs dropping from high, meant to disturb the lion cub into a state of unease and a state of unrest. Why must one try so hard to disturb? Leaches suck blood! Hearts still beat in the night. A lion cub cried praying all alone. Picked up the pieces of the broken dream memories from walking for so long alone. Carry on fortunate one, for many are not so lucky the magnificent voice rang out once more. This one true inspiration, a sweet slice of life. A flame that burns so bright. John Doe kept repeating how much a gift the lion cub was, but it was only for his own selfish glory. Turned the cub into a slave at one point while the struggle was on going with a battle of the white mountain fury. Tired and weak at the end of the night. The cub fell to bed before taking a meal. Up at first light and out the door only to be greeted with more sarcasm and injury. The cub was cheated and lied to once more. After...even still after a ride to a grand show in surprise and even a chariot ride taken care at the expense of his own castle.

The dragon answered back with more self arrogance "Alone I am better." Pay rate cut, a dying joke. A throat full of laughter, and now a swan will swallow, but will almost choke. Turkey dinner and a place to stay, though the cub could not get away. A drink had, and one, definitely one too many. The driving course could have cost lives, or time spent in the grasp of an uncle named ham, and ended in more tragedy. Fuck the lying well wisher. The cub, and his heart and mind, were dented into a swirl of emotion. Time is short, and so is the dragon, so cut the FUCKERS TAIL. This is a tale. A trial if you like, for one slimed and pissed the territorial walls. The give and the take has been weighed on the scales. Look outside the justice system walls. True blood boils hot, so hot from the day into the night. This spy that asks too many questions. One answered back openly due to the trusting ways of traits carried on from the roots of close companions. Say unto thee lay down documented flip-tuck-reverse-black magic-re-photo-videotogrophy. A trophy for your repeated speech is a memory of the mind which holds no enchantment any longer on the fragile cub heart mind. Apologies can be accepted, but like a worm gear this circle is growing tighter. The lion cub stepped out the door, he whistled a tune, and found his voice had grown mightier. The dragon was cast out of the circle for good. Allowed to walk on his sticks to paint the sky, and breathe his weak fire. Many tricks up his sleeve, though none had been shared to make the tiny lion cub grow mightier. Be gone, be gone, be gone. A song, a song, a song. A dying remembrance, let the demon be gone. Now fade out of the cubs existence. FUCK OFF FOR ONCE AND

ALL. THEY ALL GO WHOP BAM BOOM. THE CUB THUNDERDED! BE GONE AND LEAVE THE CUB TO HIS...PATH NOW YOU UNWANTED MESS. FOREVER AND EVER!!! OR ELSE! The hound slept quiet, but was ready to walk. A patient companion always ready for the hunt. Take to country for a dinner, a theater show. The greatest writer put on paper once, we all repeat you know. For it is a screen, a scream, a dream, a frame, a blame, a stage in life. A struggle we all do the best to get through. Dying for one more dying breath. A fish broke to the surface then dove back in the water to repeat the circle once more. Ground control? Looks like we are going back in. GULP. Thanks be given, and may we all be rewarded when the race car engines have lined up in a row. Horse jockeys jockey for position, but we can all be winners, it just takes a little sharing, and letting them know the intentions of the direction that you intend to go. Fuck the dragons in society, that want to breathe fire on the weak, and try to roast them for dinner and dine on their own pleasure feast. A mortal sin we can all fall prey. Constitution, inner beauty, human nature, human knowledge, it can be a living hell. Only if you let the beast wrap the finger from within, will this lucky strike light the match, and torch your mind into a terrible mind warp mind bend. Be gone to dragon children's with hidden agendas. The circle chant grew and kept repeating. The hound scent was strong, and almost mightier than that of a grizzly. In this valley of many hatred and darkened shadows. By Hallows Eve the dressed up "Billy the Kid hound" will howl out, "Regulators. Let's ride."

6/2209-6/28/09

...

Decisions. Addition. Subtraction. Sketches. Stand in lines for soup and bread. Think about it. Sick mother's children with bellies that are hungry. Needs. Wants. Jealousy. Zebra station triple zero is there really a hero that can be called super? Dragging down. Dusted. Sharing a crop with others will help to feed. Cotton is full of fiber. Who has the right to create a thread just to string someone along. Traps do little except create confusion and illusion. We can all fall. Freewill. We all have it. Amerika. An ongoing saga. Apartment doors. Dogs can attack. When not kept on leashes, and provided proper guidance. Faces. Coins. Two sides. Birds have wings. Masks can be worn. Whispers can be whispered. Spies can spy. Private eyes behind closed doors. Who is behind yours? Four walls. Safety. Bathroom stalls. Language that little kitties should not read, or should they? Have they already heard. It might just be a big news day. Tomorrow. Today. Yesterday. Laughter. Past. Present. A bow tie. Never could tie one. A first for everything. A symphony at its finest. Fine dining indeed. Shall we dance? Romance. Frivolous girls. Cougars in heat. Plates that have been filled. Lives that are complete. Waterfalls are pretty.

Wouldn't it be fun to stand under a waterfall on a beautiful warm sunny day. Exciting to think about. Grapes are sweet and they are a treat. Frozen they can even be enjoyed in a mysterious way. Ladies of the old world have a cheer about them that makes one want to run out and play like a little child on a play ground. Find those that are best friends. Make it last forever. May we all finish the rest however we decide to...

7/3/09

The Gathering

The common grounds are for the people...

To dance upon...

Shall we...

And laughter began to fill the air...

As the bodies began to sway...

And the circle was formed...

The chain was locked...

And we became ONE.

4/2/09

P.S. - It was a haunting night and smoke filled the air. She filled her sack with not a care. Her hair was wild. She was a true child. Freedom! I could feel it through the air. Thank you I called. Forever. A grateful weep as the tear water drop fall wet the paper. See you all later till' my eyes run wet yet again when a Saturday paper is delivered ahead of the regular schedule at my doorstep 'till then catch ya' 'round the next bend.

7/6/09